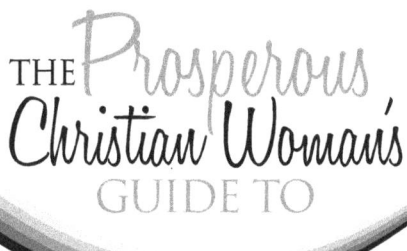

THE *Prosperous*
Christian Woman's
GUIDE TO

SPIRITUAL INTIMACY

28 DAYS TO A DEEPER, MORE
INTIMATE RELATIONSHIP WITH GOD

ILLUMINATION PRESS
Atlanta, Georgia

All scripture quotations, unless otherwise indicated, are taken from The Holy Bible, New International Version(r) NIV (r). Copyright © 1973, 1978, 1984, 2011 by Biblica, Inc. (tm)

THE PROSPEROUS CHRISTIAN WOMAN'S GUIDE TO SPIRITUAL INTIMACY

Copyright © 2018 by Benecia Ponder

All rights reserved. No part of this publication may be reproduced or transmitted in any form or by any means, including informational storage and retrieval systems, without permission in writing from the copyright holder, except for brief quotations in a review and certain other noncommercial uses permitted by copyright law.

ISBN: 978-1-7322384-4-2

Cover and Interior Design by AugustPride, LLC

ILLUMINATION PRESS
1100 Peachtree Street, Suite 250
Atlanta, Georgia 30309
United States

Welcome!

Thank you for choosing to become a part of a movement to help Christian women live happier, healthier and more prosperous lives.

For far too long Christian women have been burdened with gut-wrenching conflict—believing they have to live an "either or" life. They think things like…

Either I succeed in my career or I have a great relationship with my family.

Either I pursue my purpose or I make lots of money.

Either I live a life of faith or I live a fun, enjoyable life.

But here's my prayer for you…

Beloved, I pray that in all respects you may prosper and be in good health, just as your soul prospers.

3 John 2

I pray you prosper in every aspect of your life—spiritually, mentally, physically, and financially. I pray you prosper in your relationships and in your career. I pray you prosper in your mind, body, and soul.

The Prosperous Christian Woman is a series of devotional guides and journals to help you achieve the total life prosperity God designed you to enjoy.

Table of Contents

Get Started Here 01
God Wants A Personal Relationship With You 03
Your Relationship With God Is Personal 05
Intimacy With God Is A Process 07
How To Use This Journal 09
Week One: Know God 11
God Is Good 19
God Is Just 23
God Is Faithful 27
God Is Powerful 31
God Is Unchangeable 35
God Is Merciful 39
God Is Righteous 43
Week Two: Love God 47
God Knows Me 49
God Loves Me 53
God Forgives Me 57
God Is Gracious To Me 61
I Am A Child Of God 65

God's Love Never Ends 69

God's Love Blesses Me 73

Week Three: Trust God 77

God Will Never Leave Me 81

God Is Able 85

God Is Sovereign 89

God Keeps His Promises 93

God Is True 97

God Cares For Me 101

God Guides Me 105

God Protects Me 109

Week Four: Desire God 113

God Made Today 119

God Is Marvelous 123

God Makes Me Righteous 127

God Is Worthy Of Praise 131

God Is Wonderful 135

God Hears Me 139

I Enjoy God 143

My Intimate Moments with God 147

Get Started Here

Intimacy with God?

For a long time, it seemed like an unachievable aim to have a close, personal relationship with God. After all, how could I be intimate with someone I couldn't see, hear, or touch?

God and I couldn't go out to lunch or chat on the phone. He couldn't give me a hug when I felt sad. We couldn't go out to celebrate when I made a big accomplishment.

Even though I became a Christian at a very early age, I struggled with the feeling of separation from God for most of my life. I longed to know God on a more personal level and have a closer relationship with Him.

Can you relate?

Over the past six years, God has taken me on a journey to understand more fully what it means to have an intimate relationship with Him. I've

learned that I can indeed see, hear, and touch God. He comforts me, cheers me, and gives me strength. My relationship with God is absolutely amazing! And, while I am still growing in my relationship with God every day, I now feel closer to Him than ever before. We have a relationship that fills me with an abundance of joy and peace.

That's what I want for you—a real, intimate, and personal relationship with God.

I want to share with you some of the key insights I've learned (and am still learning) about developing intimacy with God to help you form your own personal relationship with Him.

So, before you head into the journal part of this book, here are some key things to keep in mind.

God Wants A Personal Relationship With You

When we consider how awesome and amazing God is, it is easy to feel unworthy to even be in His presence, let alone have a close personal relationship With Him.

Why would the powerful and mighty Creator of the Universe want a relationship with us? David asked the same question in Psalm 8:3-4.

> When I look at the night sky and see the work of Your fingers—
> the moon and the stars You set in place—
> what are mere mortals
> that You should think about them,
> human beings that You
> should care for them?

Although it can seem quite unimaginable at times, God wants us to have a close relationship with Him. He wants that relationship with us so much that He sent Jesus to die on the cross for us.

Your Relationship With God is Personal

Please don't allow the subtitle of this book to mislead you into believing that there is some prescription or formula that every Christian should follow to establish a closer relationship with God.

Quite the contrary. I pray that you will use this book to connect with God in your own unique way. The insights I'm sharing are designed to spark your personal conversations with Him.

Intimacy With God is a Process

Although our culture has become littered with examples of instant relationships, establishing true intimacy is a process. In fact, there are four phases to establishing intimacy God—Know God, Love God, Trust God, and Desire God.

As you move through each phase of this process, you will grow deeper in your intimacy with God.

How To Use This Journal

This book is designed to be a 28-day journey to greater intimacy with God. The journey is broken into four phases—Know God, Love God, Trust God and Desire God, Enjoy God. At the beginning of each week, you'll find a brief study on the week's focus. The weeks are then broken down into daily journey.

Each day's journal section contains a scripture to mediate on as well as a place to reflect and journal.

At the end of the book, there is a place for you to record your special intimate moments with God.

WEEK ONE
Know God

"I keep asking that the God of our Lord Jesus Christ, the glorious Father, may give you the Spirit of wisdom and revelation, so that you may know Him better."

Ephesians 1:17 (NIV)

Do you know God?

Before you answer with a quick "yes", really ponder the question. I'm not just asking you if you know that God exits. Of course, you do... you wouldn't be reading this if you didn't.

I'm asking you if you really know God. And, don't be ashamed if you're not sure or if your answer is that you don't know God as well as you would like to.

Many Christian women (even those super spiritual, super holy ones) don't really know God. Even after being in church for years, they still only have a casual acquaintance with Him.

But, I imagine you're reading this because you want more. You desire a deeper, more intimate relationship with God.

You are starting in the right place because knowing God is the first step to that kind of relationship with Him.

How to Know God Better

There are lots of different opinions about how to know God better. Some gurus say you should engage in intense self-reflection and examine who you are because God lives in you. Some say you should study all the world religions and find the common denominators to tell you about who God really is. I've even heard people say intellectual inquiry is the way to know God. They say philosophy is the best path to knowing God.

I disagree with them all.

To explain why, I'll use a very practical analogy…

Let's say you meet a guy you want to get to know better. How do you do it?

Do you ask yourself what he likes, what he does for a living, where he went to school? Of course not. How would you know unless he tells you?

Would you go and talk to 10 other guys and ask

them to tell you about who they are? Absolutely not. All that would do is tell you about them not the guy you're trying to get to know.

Would you go to the library and read lots of books on how to think about dating? Not at all. Knowing about dating won't tell you what you want to know about him.

So, how do you get to know him? You ask him. You spend time with him.

That's exactly how we get to know God. And, the great part about it is God has revealed Himself to us through the Scriptures and He has given us the Holy Spirit to truly know and understand Him.

The biggest problem with all those other ways of knowing God is that we make God look like what we think He should look like and we don't take the time to discover who He really is. Those other methods are exercises in self-effort and all we're able to come up with is a distorted incomplete picture of God.

In this first phase of your journey to greater intimacy with God, you're going to get to know Him better by looking at what His Word says about Him.

But, before you start getting to know God better, consider this...

What Kind Of Relationship Do You Want?

There are lots of different opinions about how to know God better. Some gurus say you should engage in intense self-reflection and examine who you are because God lives in you. Some say you should study all the world religions and find the common denominators to tell you about who God really is. I've even heard people say intellectual inquiry is the way to know God. They say philosophy is the best path to knowing God.

I disagree with them all.

To explain why, I'll use a very practical analogy…

Let's say you meet a guy you want to get to know better. How do you do it?

Do you ask yourself what he likes, what he does for a living, where he went to school? Of course not. How would you know unless he tells you?

Would you go and talk to 10 other guys and ask them to tell you about who they are? Absolutely not. All that would do is tell you about them not the guy you're trying to get to know.

Would you go to the library and read lots of books on how to think about dating? Not at all. Knowing about dating won't tell you what you want to know about him.

So, how do you get to know him? You ask him. You spend time with him.

That's exactly how we get to know God. And, the great part about it is God has revealed Himself to us through the Scriptures and He

has given us the Holy Spirit to truly know and understand Him.

The biggest problem with all those other ways of knowing God is that we make God look like what we think He should look like and we don't take the time to discover who He really is. Those other methods are exercises in self-effort and all we're able to come up with is a distorted incomplete picture of God.

In this first phase of your journey to greater intimacy with God, you're going to get to know Him better by looking at what His Word says about Him.

But, before you start getting to know God better, consider this...

Date: _____

GOD IS GOOD

"For You, O Lord, are good and forgiving, abounding in steadfast love to all who call upon You."

- Psalm 86:5 -

REFLECTIONS
How has God been good to you?

Date: _____

GOD IS JUST

"Therefore, the LORD waits to be gracious to you, and therefore He exalts Himself to show mercy to you. For the LORD is a God of justice; blessed are all those who wait for Him."

- Isaiah 30:18 -

REFLECTIONS

How has God been just (fair, kind) to you?

_____
_____
_____
_____
_____
_____
_____
_____
_____
_____
_____
_____
_____
_____
_____
_____
_____
_____
_____
_____

Date: _____

GOD IS FAITHFUL

"Know therefore that the LORD your God is God; He is the faithful God, keeping His covenant of love to a thousand generations of those who love Him and keep His commandments."

- Deuteronomy 7:9 -

REFLECTIONS
How has God been faithful to you?

Date: _____

GOD IS POWERFUL

"Ah Lord God! Behold, You have made the heavens and the earth by Your great power and by Your outstretched arm! Nothing is too difficult for You."

- Jeremiah 32:17 -

REFLECTIONS

How has God been powerful in your life?

Date: _____

GOD IS UNCHANGEABLE

"I the LORD do not change. So, you, the descendants of Jacob, are not destroyed."

- Malachi 3:6 -

REFLECTIONS

How has God been unchangeable in your life?

Date: _____

GOD IS MERCIFUL

"But Thou, O Lord, art a God merciful and gracious, slow to anger and abundant in lovingkindness and truth."

- Psalm 86:15 -

REFLECTIONS

How has God been merciful to you?

Date: _____

GOD IS RIGHTEOUS

"The LORD is righteous in all His ways And kind in all His deeds."

- Psalm 145:17 -

REFLECTIONS
How has God been righteous to you?

WEEK TWO
Love God

"I pray that you, being rooted and established in love, may have power, together with all the saints, to grasp how wide and long and high and deep is the love of Christ, and to know this love that surpasses knowledge–that you may be filled to the measure of all the fullness of God."

Ephesians 3:17-19

To know God is to love Him.

To know God is to love Him.

That statement might sound a bit trivial—but think about it for a moment.

What happened over the past week as you delved into getting to know God better?

I'm certain that the more you began to discover and reflect on the attributes of God's character, the deeper your love grew. And, this is true even if you started this journey with a deep love for God already.

The more you reflect on God's goodness, His character, and His love for you, the more love you have for Him.

Date: _____

GOD KNOWS ME

"O Lord, You have searched me and known me. You know when I sit down and when I rise; You understand my thought from afar. You scrutinize my path and my lying down And are intimately acquainted with all my ways."

- Psalm 139:1-3 -

REFLECTIONS
What does it mean that God knows you?
How does that make you feel?

Date: _____

GOD LOVES ME

"... God showed His great love for us by sending Christ to die for us while we were still sinners."

- Romans 5:8 -

REFLECTIONS

*God knows you and He loves you.
Meditate on that and then d write a prayer of praise.*

Date: _____

GOD FORGIVES ME

"… In Your love You kept me from the pit of destruction; You have put all my sins behind Your back."

- Isaiah 38:17 -

REFLECTIONS

Think about all the times God has forgiven you. Praise Him!

Date: _____

GOD IS GRACIOUS TO ME

"... because of His great love for us, God, who is rich in mercy, made us alive with Christ even when we were dead in transgressions—it is by grace you have been saved."

- Ephesians 2:4,5 -

REFLECTIONS
How has God been gracious to you?

Date: _____

I AM CHILD OF GOD

"How great is the love the Father has lavished on us, that we should be called children of God!"

- 1 John 3:1 -

REFLECTIONS

What does it mean to you to be a child of God?

Date: _____

GOD'S LOVE NEVER ENDS

"Give thanks to the LORD Almighty, for the LORD is good; His love endures forever."

- Jeremiah 33:11 -

REFLECTIONS

Meditate on today's scripture. Write a prayer of praise.

Date: _____

GOD'S LOVE BLESSES ME

"Live in such a way that God's love can bless you as you wait for the eternal life that our Lord Jesus Christ in His mercy is going to give you."

- Jude 1:21 -

REFLECTIONS

How can you open up to receive more of God's blessings?

WEEK THREE
Trust God

"I keep asking that the God of our Lord Jesus Christ, the glorious Father, may give you the Spirit of wisdom and revelation, so that you may know Him better."

Ephesians 1:17 (NIV)

The cornerstone if any solid relationship is trust.

Think about your relationship with your best friend for a moment. Would she be your best friend if you couldn't trust her with your secrets? What about your significant other—would you continue in a relationship with him if you thought he would betray your trust?

Of course not.

The same is true of your relationship with God. To truly have an intimate relationship with Him, you've got to trust Him with all your heart.

But sometimes it's difficult. Not because God isn't worthy of our trust but because we have sinned against Him.

Tell God All About It

Have you ever wronged someone and felt guilty about it?

I remember a time a while ago when I borrowed

something from my mom and lost it. When she couldn't find it a few days later, she asked everyone in the house if we had seen it. I said "no" right along with everyone else.

The guilt of that lie weighed on me for a long time and it made me feel distant from my mom. I wanted to tell her the truth but was afraid that she would think less of ne. She didn't treat me any differently, but our relationship suffered because I became more distant.

My guilt and shame caused me to be guarded and I didn't feel as close to her as I used to. It wasn't until I trusted our relationship and her love enough to tell the truth that I was able to feel close to my mom again.

The same thing happens in our relationship with God. The difference is God already knows about everything we have ever done. However, He wants us to trust Him and His love for us enough that we confess our sins to Him.

When you hold on to unrepented sins and the

guilt and shame associated with them, you block the free flow of trust in your relating hip with God.

Remember, nothing can separate you from the love of God—not even your sin.

Date: _____

GOD WILL NEVER LEAVE ME

"Suppose I were to rise with the sun in the east. Suppose I travel to the west where it sinks into the ocean. Your hand would always be there to guide me. Your right hand would still be holding me close."

- Psalm 139:9-10 -

REFLECTIONS

How has God shown up in various situations in your life?

_____
_____
_____
_____
_____
_____
_____
_____
_____
_____
_____
_____
_____
_____
_____
_____
_____
_____
_____
_____
_____
_____
_____

Date: _____

GOD IS ABLE

"I am the LORD the God of all mankind. Is anything too hard for Me?"

- Jeremiah 32:27 -

REFLECTIONS

Knowing that God is able to handle anything and everything, what is it time to trust Him to do in your life?

Date: _____

GOD IS SOVEREIGN

"Ah, Sovereign LORD, You have made the heavens and the earth by Your great power and outstretched arm. Nothing is too hard for You."

- Jeremiah 32:17 -

REFLECTIONS

What have you been trying to control in your life? How can you let go and give it to God?

Date: _____

GOD KEEPS HIS PROMISES

"Without wavering, let us hold tightly to the hope we say we have, for God can be trusted to keep His promise."

- Hebrews 10:23 -

REFLECTIONS

Knowing that God keeps His promises—what promises has God given you that you are ready to more fully believe?

Date: _____

GOD IS TRUE

"For the word of the LORD holds true and everything He does is worthy of our trust."

- Psalm 33:4 -

REFLECTIONS

Think back...How has God's Word been proven true in your life?

Date: _____

GOD CARES FOR ME

"Cast all your anxiety on Him because He cares for you."

- 1 Peter 5:7 -

REFLECTIONS

*Meditate on today's scripture.
Write a prayer to give your cares to God.*

Date: _____

GOD GUIDES ME

"The LORD leads with unfailing love and faithfulness all those who keep His covenant and obey His decrees."

- Psalm 25:10 -

REFLECTIONS

Write a prayer asking for Gods guidance through a situation you are dealing with.

Date: _____

GOD PROTECTS ME

"The LORD is my light and my salvation—so why should I be afraid? The LORD protects me from danger—so why should I tremble?"

- Psalm 27:1 -

REFLECTIONS

*Meditate on today's scripture.
Write a declaration of God's protection over your life.*

WEEK FOUR
Desire God

*"As the deer pants for streams of water,
so my soul pants for you, my God.
My soul thirsts for God, for the living God.
When can I go and meet with God?"*

Psalm 42:1-2

How strong is your desire for God?

The answer to that question more than likely depends on how long you've been a Christian. In the beginning there is great excitement and our desire for Him is quite strong.

However, over time, the spark and fire we have for God dies down. We become complacent and take God for granted.

Intimacy With God Is A Lifelong Pursuit

Developing intimacy with God is not something you do once and have it for the rest of your life.

Although you can never lose your salvation and place as God's child, the level of closeness you feel with Him can diminish if you aren't diligent in maintain your desire for Him.

Over the last three weeks, you've been very intentional about setting aside time to spend with God. You've made deepening your knowledge, love, and trust for God a regular part of your

day. Don't lose that.

Nurturing your intimacy with God is a whole lot easier than trying to re-establish it after you've let it grow stagnant.

Let me share with you two key ways to keep your relationship with God vibrant.

Enjoy God

Be careful not to let spending time with God become just another item you check off your to do list. You certainly want to spend regular time with God but make it interesting.

You might add praise and worship songs to your daily devotional tine. Maybe you have a regular "date with God" where you enjoy a delicious meal while reflecting on all things you're grateful for. A few weeks ago, I spent quality time with God as I walked on the beach watching the sunrise. There are many ways to spend time with God. The most important thing is to have fun and enjoy Him.

Make God Your Priority

It's very easy to neglect your relationship with God. After all, you have lots of demands on your time. Between your family, work, and multitude of other commitments it can be easy to sacrifice your time with God. Missing a day of devotion here or there becomes missing a week or a month.

Your relationship with God must not be a priority in your life, it must be the priority. You show how much you desire God by the quality of investment you make in spending time with Him. It's definitely the case that your actions speak louder than words.

Do you carve out time every day to be with God?

Do you think about your relationship with God throughout the day?

Does God get the best hours of your day or do you give Him what's left over?

Are you willing to invest financial resources on things that

will enhance your relationship with God?

Does your concern about what other people might think hinder your relationship with god?

Ask the Holy Spirit to make your relationship with God the highest priority in your life.

Date: _____

GOD MADE TODAY

"This is the day the LORD has made. We will rejoice and be glad in it."

- Psalm 118:24 -

REFLECTIONS

How can you enjoy your time with God more?

Date: _____

GOD IS MARVELOUS

*"Praise be to the LORD God,
the God of Israel,
who alone does marvelous deeds."*

- Psalm 72:18 -

REFLECTIONS
How has God been marvelous in your life?

Date: _____

GOD MAKES ME RIGHTEOUS

"I delight greatly in the LORD; my soul rejoices in my God. For He has clothed me with garments of salvation and arrayed me in a robe of righteousness"

- Isaiah 61:10 -

REFLECTIONS
Praise God for making you righteous.

Date: _____

GOD IS WORTHY OF PRAISE

*"Great is the LORD!
He is most worthy of praise!
His greatness is beyond discovery!
How great is our Lord!
His power is absolute!
His understanding i
beyond comprehension!"*

- Psalm 145:3,5 -

REFLECTIONS

Praise God! Use the space below to write all the things for which you can praise God.

Date: _____

GOD IS WONDERFUL

"Think of the wonderful works He has done, the miracles, and the judgments He handed down,"

- 1 Chronicles 16:12 -

REFLECTIONS
How has God been wonderful to you?

Date: _____

GOD HEARS ME

"Before they call I will answer; while they are still speaking I will hear."

- Isaiah 65:24 -

REFLECTIONS
Talk to God about what is on your mind.

Date: _____

I ENJOY GOD

"For in Him we live and move and have our being."

- Acts 17:28 -

REFLECTIONS

In what ways will you continue to enjoy your relationship with God?

My Intimate Moments With God

Use this section to record and journal about your special intimate moments with God.

Date: _____

Date: _____

Date: _____

Date: _____

Date: _____

Date: _____

Date: _____

Date: _____

Date: _____

Date: _____

Date: _____

Date: _____

Date: _____

Date: _____

Date: _____

Date: _____

Date: _____

Date: _____

Date: _____

Date: _____

Date: _____

Date: _____

Date: _____

Date: _____

Date: _____

Date: _____

Date: _____

Date: _____

www.ingramcontent.com/pod-product-compliance
Lightning Source LLC
LaVergne TN
LVHW040115080426
835507LV00039B/280